COMMUNITY · CONNECTIONS

?

HOW DOES IT FLY?
JET PLANE

BY MATT MULLINS

Published in the United States of America by Cherry Lake Publishing
Ann Arbor, Michigan
www.cherrylakepublishing.com

Content Adviser: Jacob Zeiger, Production Support Engineer, the Boeing Company

Photo Credits: Cover and page 1, ©Carlos E. Santa Maria/Shutterstock, Inc.;
page 5, ©iStockphoto/icholakov; page 7, ©RenataFedosova/Shutterstock, Inc.;
page 9, ©Pincasso/Shutterstock, Inc.; page 11, ©Talyzov Alexey/Shutterstock, Inc.;
page 13, ©Igor Dolgov/Dreamstime.com; page 15, Stocktrek Images, Inc./Alamy;
page 17, ©iStockphoto/choja; page 19, ©iStockphoto/sjlocke;
page 21, ©Gary718/Dreamstime.com.

LIBRARY OF CONGRESS CATALOGING-IN-PUBLICATION DATA
Mullins, Matt.
  How does it fly? Jet plane/by Matt Mullins.
    p. cm.—(Community connections)
  Includes bibliographical references and index.
  ISBN-13: 978-1-61080-069-3 (library binding)
  ISBN-10: 1-61080-069-9 (library binding)
  1. Jet planes—Juvenile literature. I. Title. II. Title: Jet plane.
  TL547.M75 2011
  629.133'349—dc22   2010051585

Cherry Lake Publishing would like to acknowledge the
work of The Partnership for 21st Century Skills. Please
visit www.21stcenturyskills.org for more information.

Printed in the United States of America
Corporate Graphics Inc.
July 2011
CLFA09

JET PLANE

CONTENTS

4 **What Is a Jet Plane?**

8 **How Does a Jet Plane Fly?**

12 **The Biggest Jet Planes**

16 **A Helpful Crew**

22 Glossary

23 Find Out More

24 Index

24 About the Author

HOW DOES IT FLY?

WHAT IS A JET PLANE?

You hear it roar overhead when you're near an airport. You see it high in the sky. It leaves trails of white clouds. It is a big, fast jet plane. Do you know why it's called a jet? Because it has **jet engines**. These engines usually hang from the wings.

How many jet engines do you see on this jet plane?

Jets are very big. They have a lot of things to carry. They carry a lot of people. They carry plenty of gasoline for the engines. They carry food and drinks. They also carry **luggage**. Sometimes they even carry passengers' pets!

Passengers sit in rows of seats. Some luggage is kept in bins above their heads.

When you walk onto a jet plane, look at all the seats. Guess how many people can ride in the jet. Did you include the people who work on the plane, called the **crew**? Ask a crew member. Did you guess correctly?

7

HOW DOES A JET PLANE FLY?

Jet planes fly even though they are heavy. Jet engines give the plane **thrust**. Thrust moves the plane through the air. Wings provide **lift**. Their shape makes the air push the plane up. The faster the engine moves the plane, the more the air pushes up!

A jet plane must gain speed to take off.

Pay attention the next time you are near a jet plane. Look at its engines and wings. Which is bigger, the front or the back of the engine? How is the top of the wing shaped differently than the bottom?

Engines take in air through a wide, open front. They add fuel to the air and burn it. The heated air escapes through the smaller back of the engine. This moves the plane forward.

A wing's shape makes air go fast on top. Air moves slowly underneath. This causes lift.

The shape of the wings and engines are important in controlling how a jet plane flies.

THE BIGGEST JET PLANES

Not all jet planes carry people and luggage. Some carry **cargo**. This includes trucks, big containers, or big machine parts. The largest cargo plane in the world is the Antonov An-225. Its **wingspan** is about as long as a football field!

This plane's nose can lift up so containers or other items can be loaded onto it.

The An-225 and other cargo planes also carry supplies to areas hit by disasters. This usually includes food and medicine.

Very large cargo planes might even carry other planes! The An-225 is just one example. The 747 is another. NASA used 747s to carry the space shuttles.

NASA's 747 Shuttle Carriers took shuttles from their launch and landing sites.

THINK!

Airports have runways. Planes land and take off from runways. Runways are long and wide. Why do you think they are so long? Why so wide? Why do big airports have many runways?

15

A HELPFUL CREW

Jet planes do not fly themselves.
A crew of people operates a jet
plane. The pilot flies the plane.
Other trained people help make
sure the plane's systems operate
correctly. They also help steer
and locate places the plane
must go.

A copilot helps the pilot fly and keep track of
the plane's systems.

Flight attendants help passengers. Flight attendants bring food and drinks and answer questions. They also make sure passengers keep their seat belts on.

Ground crews load luggage onto planes. They put fuel in the plane. They show pilots where to go when the plane is on the ground.

A flight attendant hands out lunch to passengers.

Jet planes can be huge. It takes a lot of people to operate them! Pilots, flight attendants, and other crew members need training. They learn how the plane works. They practice what to do if something goes wrong.

Are you interested in jet planes? Maybe one day you could become a member of the crew!

A ground crew member helps a jet pilot see which way to go.

Flying machines have been around longer than you might think. Ask a librarian or teacher about the earliest flying machines. How did people begin to fly? Ask for help to learn about this, too.

21

GLOSSARY

cargo (KAR-goh) items carried by planes, cars, trucks, and ships

crew (KROO) the people who work together on a machine or project

flight attendants (FLITE uh-TEN-duhntss) people who serve passengers on an airplane

jet engines (JET EHN-juhnz) engines that produce motion as a result of pushing hot gases out of the back of the engine

lift (LIFT) the upward force of flight

luggage (LUH-gihj) containers that hold a traveler's belongings

thrust (THRUHST) the forward force of flight

wingspan (WING-span) the distance between the outer tip of one wing and the outer tip of the opposite wing

FIND OUT MORE

BOOKS

Braulick, Carrie A. *Jets*. Mankato, MN: Capstone Press, 2007.

Eason, Sarah. *How Does a Jet Plane Work?* New York: Gareth Stevens Publishing, 2010.

Goldish, Meish. *Freaky-Big Airplanes*. New York: Bearport Publishing, 2010.

WEB SITES

Idaho Public Television: Dialogue for Kids—Flight
http://idahoptv.org/dialogue4kids/season9/flight/
Watch a video and find tons of information and activities about flight.

NASA: Ultra-Efficient Engine Technology Kid's Page
www.ueet.nasa.gov/StudentSite/
Play games and read about how planes fly and the history of flight.

INDEX

air, 8, 10
airports, 4, 15
An-225 cargo
    plane, 12, 14

cargo, 6, 12, 14
crew members, 7,
    16, 18, 20

drinks, 6, 18

engines, 4, 6, 8,
    9, 10

flight attendants,
    18, 20
flying machines, 21
food, 6, 14, 18
fuel, 6, 10, 18

ground crews, 18

lift, 8, 10
luggage, 6, 12, 18

passengers, 6, 7, 18
pets, 6
pilots, 16, 18, 20

runways, 15

seat belts, 18
seats, 7
shapes, 8, 9, 10
sizes, 6, 9, 12, 20
speed, 8, 10

thrust, 8
training, 16, 20

wings, 4, 8, 9, 10
wingspan, 12

ABOUT THE AUTHOR

Matt Mullins lives
near an airport in
Madison, Wisconsin.
Matt has a master's
degree in the history
of science and writes
about all sorts of
things—science,
technology, business,
academics, food, and
more. He also writes
and directs films and
spends time with
his son.